The Locked Room and Other Horror Stories

M. R. JAMES

Level 4

Retold by Louise Greenwood and Carolyn Jones
Series Editors: Andy Hopkins and Jocelyn Potter

Pearson Education Limited
Edinburgh Gate, Harlow,
Essex CM20 2JE, England
and Associated Companies throughout the world.

ISBN 0 582 41807 0

'The Ash-Tree','A School Story','The Diary of Mr Poynter'
('The Curtains'),'An Evening's Entertainment' ('The Flies'), 'Rats'
('The Locked Room'),'The Mezzotint' ('The Painting of —ngley Hall'),'Lost Hearts',
'Martin's Close' (Martin's Lake'),and 'The Tractate Middoth' ('The Two Cousins'),
first published by Edward Arnold 1931
This adaptation first published by Penguin Books 1993
Published by Addison Wesley Longman Limited and Penguin Books Ltd. 1998
New edition first published 1999

7 9 10 8 6

Text copyright © Louise Greenwood and Carolyn Jones 1993
Illustrations copyright © Piers Sandford 1993
All rights reserved

The moral right of the adapters and of the illustrator has been asserted

Typeset by Digital Type, London
Set in 11/14pt Bembo
Printed in China
SWTC/06

Published by Pearson Education Limited in association with
Penguin Books Ltd, both companies being subsidiaries of Pearson Plc

For a complete list of titles available in the Penguin Readers series, please write to your local
Pearson Education office or to: Penguin Readers Marketing Department,
Pearson Education, Edinburgh Gate, Harlow, Essex CM20 2JE.

Contents

Introduction

He jumped and screamed and, as he did, the face of the thing came up towards him: no eyes, no nose, no mouth. He screamed again and rushed to the door. He felt the thing touch his back and start to tear at his shirt . . .

Things . . . things in the night, things in the house, screaming, running, staring . . . In these stories there are things that are worse than your worst dreams.

Giant black spiders living in a tree. The terrible ghost that waits outside a window. Empty clothes that walk. The strange thin woman who moves through a man's picture. The boy with the long, dirty fingernails – and a hole in his chest. The woman who screams from the bottom of a lake. And the dry dusty old man who reads – but has no eyes!

Here are nine stories like no others you have read.

Montague Rhodes James was born in 1862 in a village in Kent, in the south of England, where his father was a vicar. From an early age, he loved old books and studied history, the Bible, languages and the books of past centuries at Cambridge University. He studied, lived and worked at the University from 1882 to 1918.

He began to write ghost and horror stories after reading the stories of Irish writer Sheridan Le Fanu. From the early 1890s, he read one of his own stories to friends at Christmas every year. His great knowledge of history gave his stories an unusual amount of detail and his ghosts seem more real, and are more frightening, than those of almost any other writer.

M. R. James died in 1936.

Chapter 1   The Ash-Tree

Visitors to Castringham Hall in Suffolk will find it almost unchanged from the days when our story took place. They can still see the beautiful old house with its gardens and lake. However, the one thing missing is the ash-tree, which used to stand, proud and tall, in front of the house, its branches almost touching the walls.

This story begins in 1690 with a strange, lonely old woman, Mrs Mothersole, who was found guilty of being a witch. Sir Matthew Fell, the owner of Castringham Hall at that time, described how she used to climb into the ash-tree outside his bedroom every time there was a full moon. He said that she usually carried a strange knife to cut off parts of the tree and that she talked to herself. Once he followed her home, but she disappeared and when he knocked on the door of her house, she came downstairs in her night clothes looking sleepy. He and the villagers agreed that it was certain she did these things by magic and so she was hanged. Before she died, she fought and shouted, and her last strange words were: 'There will be guests at the Hall.'

After the hanging, Sir Matthew felt uncomfortable and guilty, and he told his friend the vicar about his worries. 'You did the right thing, Sir Matthew,' were the wise words of the vicar. 'I'm sure she was a dangerous woman.' Sir Matthew felt happier.

That evening, Sir Matthew and the vicar went for a walk in the gardens of Castringham Hall. It was the night of the full moon. As they were returning to the house, Sir Matthew pointed to the ash-tree in great surprise. 'What kind of animal is that running down the ash-tree? It looks very strange.'

The vicar only saw the moving animal for a moment, but he thought that it had more than four legs. He shook his head. 'I

1

'What kind of animal is that running down the ash-tree? It looks very strange.'

must be tired,' he thought to himself. 'After all, what animal has more than four legs?' He said nothing to Sir Matthew, but just wished him good night.

The next morning, Sir Matthew's servants were surprised not to find him downstairs at his usual time of six o'clock. When seven o'clock and then eight o'clock passed, they began to suspect that something was terribly wrong and they went up to his bedroom. The door was locked. After knocking several times and still getting no answer from inside, they broke down the door and entered, to find that their fears were right. Sir Matthew's body lay on the bed, dead and completely black. There were no wounds or other marks on him and everything in the room looked as usual, except that the window was wide open. His servants at first suspected poison but the doctor who was called found no such thing and could offer no real explanation for Sir Matthew's death.

When he heard the news, the vicar rushed to Castringham Hall, and, while he was waiting to hear the doctor's opinion, he looked at Sir Matthew's Bible, which was lying on a table by the dead man's bedside. He opened the book and the first words he read were from the book of Luke, chapter 8: 'Cut it down' were the words he read.

◆

The servants locked Sir Matthew's room that day and it stayed locked up for the next forty years. By that time, Sir Richard Fell, Sir Matthew's grandson, was living at Castringham Hall. He enjoyed spending money, especially on rebuilding parts of the Hall. He also decided to make the local church bigger so that his family could have a fine new seat in the new part of the church. In order to complete this building work, some of the graves in the graveyard had to be moved. One of the graves was that of Mrs Mothersole, the old witch who began this story. The villagers were excited about the opening of her grave and a crowd came to watch. However, they and the workmen were amazed to find the grave completely empty: no body, no bones, no dust.

At about this time, Sir Richard started to sleep very badly. The wind made his fire smoke and the curtains move and, because his room faced east, the sun woke him up early in the morning. One morning he asked his servant to help him choose a better room and he made a tour of the house, finding something wrong with each room. Each one was either too cold or too noisy or it faced the wrong direction. Finally, he found himself outside his grandfather's old room. His servant tried to persuade him not to go in:

'It's a bad room, sir. They say terrible things happened in there, and no one has opened the door since the death of your grandfather. Also, the ash-tree is right outside the window and that's always unlucky, sir.'

But Sir Richard was not listening. He unlocked the door and walked straight in. 'See? Nothing unusual in here, James!' he said and he opened the window. As he did so, he noticed how tall and dark the ash-tree was. Its branches seemed to be trying to reach into the room. But he said nothing.

At that moment, a stranger rang the bell at the front door of the Hall. The servant brought him up to the bedroom, where Sir Richard was standing, looking around him at the old paintings and old books. 'I must apologize for interrupting you, Sir Richard,' said the stranger, 'but please allow me to introduce myself. My name is William Crome. My grandfather was the vicar here in your grandfather's time. I have some papers to deliver to you.'

'Delighted to meet you,' said Sir Richard. 'James, please bring us some wine in the library and then move my clothes and things into this room for me. I will sleep here in future.'

While he was drinking a glass of wine with William Crome in the library, Sir Richard looked at the papers, many of which belonged to his grandfather. Among them he found the notes made by the old vicar about the day of Sir Matthew's mysterious death.

'Well, well,' said Sir Richard, laughing quietly. 'How very interesting! It seems that my grandfather's Bible gave a piece of advice on the day he died and your grandfather thought it could be about that old ash-tree outside the bedroom window – "Cut it down" the Good Book told him. Those were the first words your grandfather saw when he opened the Bible on the day of my grandfather's death.'

'Do you still have that old Bible?' asked William Crome, 'I'd very much like to see it.'

Sir Richard found the old Bible easily. 'Yes, here it is. A bit dusty, I'm afraid. Let's see what it has to tell me. I'll open it at any page and read the first words I see, just as your grandfather did.'

He opened the book and his eyes fell on the words, 'You shall look for me in the morning, and I shall not be here.' Sir Richard was sure that the words were again about the ash-tree – the Bible was trying to give him some advice! He ordered some of his servants to cut it down the next day.

◆

But Sir Richard did not live to see them cut the ash-tree down. That night, at exactly midnight, a strange and terrible animal jumped from Sir Richard's bed, ran silently to the window and disappeared into the shadowy branches of the enormous tree. No one was there to see it but the next morning they found Sir Richard's body, like his grandfather's, dead and completely black.

When William Crome heard the news of his new friend's death, the words from the Bible came back to him: 'You shall look for me in the morning and I shall not be here.' He immediately hurried to Castringham Hall, where he found the family and servants crowded round the ash-tree.

'Sir Richard's last orders were that we should cut down this tree,' explained James and then, in a quieter voice, he went on, 'and there's something very strange about that tree, sir. Very strange. It's hollow and they say something lives inside it.'

The gardener put his ladder against the tree and climbed up to look inside. As he held a light over the hole, his face suddenly looked so terrified that several of the people watching from below screamed and turned to run. The gardener himself fell off the ladder, dropping his lamp down into the hollow tree, which quickly caught fire. As the tree started to burn, the crowd saw an animal run from the tree. They screamed in horror as they saw its shape and size. It looked like an enormous spider, about the same size as a man's head and covered all over with grey hair.

'Look, there's another! And another!' someone shouted. For a long time the men watched these terrifying animals trying to escape from the fire one after another, and then they killed them with sticks.

*As the tree started to burn, the crowd   saw an animal run
from the tree.*

At last, the fire burned itself out and William Crome, James the servant and some of the braver people went to look inside the blackened tree. There they found the bones of a human being. The doctors who examined it afterwards said that it was the body of a woman who died around 1690 ... the year that old Mrs Mothersole was hanged.

Chapter 2   A School Story

Two men, John and Edgar, were having dinner together one night when a conversation started on the subject of school-days. One of them, John, told the following strange story:

'When I went to the school in September of 1870, I immediately became friendly with a Scottish boy called McLeod. It was a large school and the teachers changed quite often. One term a new teacher named Sampson came to teach at the school. He taught us Latin. He was tall and pale with a black beard and he was popular with the boys because he used to tell us all about his travels to different countries. He always carried an old gold coin in is pocket, which he found on a trip to Turkey, and one day he let us look at this coin closely. On one side of it was the head of a king – I don't know which one – and on the other side of it were the letters G.W.S. (for Sampson's name) and the date 24 July 1865.

We enjoyed Sampson's classes because he often asked us to invent sentences of our own, instead of always doing the boring exercises in the grammar book. One day, he asked us for sentences using the word 'remember' in Latin. We all wrote our sentences in the usual way, and Sampson came round to correct each of us. My friend McLeod seemed to be having some difficulty in thinking of a sentence and when the bell went for break, I saw him write something very quickly, just before Sampson reached him. So McLeod's sentence was the last one that Sampson corrected that day; I waited outside the classroom for what seemed a long time before my friend at last came out. I guessed that he was in trouble for making a mistake. When he did come out, he was looking thoughtful.

'What happened? Was old Sampson angry?' I asked.

'No. My sentence was all right, I think. I wrote "Memento putei inter quattuor taxos",' said McLeod.

'Well, what does all that mean?' I asked.

'That's the funny thing,' he explained. 'I don't really know, you see. I couldn't think of anything to write until just before Sampson got to me. Then those words just came into my head from nowhere and – it was very strange – I could see a sort of picture of it in my head. I think it means "Remember the well among the four trees". When Sampson read it he went quiet for a long time, then he started to ask me questions about my family and where I came from. Then he let me go.'

We soon forgot about the lesson and McLeod's strange sentence because the next day McLeod became ill with a cold and he didn't come to school for a week. Nothing happened for about a month, until one day when we were, again, writing Latin sentences for Sampson. This time we had to write them on pieces of paper and give them to him for correction. He started looking through them, but when he got to one piece of paper he turned white and cried out, looking very frightened. He got up and hurried out of the classroom and we sat there for a long time, wondering what to do. Finally, I got up to have a look at the papers and the first thing I noticed was that the top one was in red ink. Our school never allowed us to use red ink; it was against the rules. The sentence on the paper said 'Si tu non veneris ad me, ego veniam ad te', which means 'If you don't come to me, I will come to you'. All the boys looked at it and they all promised that the sentence was not theirs. To check, I counted the pieces of paper – there were seventeen of them ... but there were only sixteen boys in the class. Where this paper came from, no one could say. I put it in my pocket and it wasn't until that afternoon that I took it out again: it was completely white, with no sign of the red writing on it anywhere! I know it was the same piece of paper because I could still see my fingermarks on it. Anyway, Sampson eventually came back at the end of that lesson and told us we could go. He looked at the papers one by one, and probably thought it was his imagination playing tricks. He looked pale and worried.

The next day, Sampson was in school again and he seemed quite normal, but it was that night that the third strange thing happened. It was about midnight when I suddenly woke up; somebody was shouting at me. It was McLeod, who shared my room; he looked terrified. 'Quick,' he said, 'I think a burglar is trying to get into Sampson's room.' I rushed to the window but could see nothing. Somehow, though, I felt that something *was* wrong out there and the two of us waited, watching closely.

'Tell me exactly what you saw or heard,' I whispered.

'I didn't hear anything but about five minutes before I woke you I just found myself standing here at the window,' McLeod whispered back. 'There was a terrible-looking man standing just outside Sampson's window. He was very tall and very thin . . . and . . . he didn't really look like a living person at all. More like a ghost. He seemed to be making a sign to Sampson to go with him. That's all I saw before I woke you up.'

We waited a long time, watching, but we saw nothing more that night. Everything was quiet outside. We woke up feeling tired and strange in the morning. But during the day the news went round that no one could find Sampson anywhere, and he didn't come for our Latin class that day. In fact, we never heard of or saw Sampson again. Somehow, McLeod and I knew that we should keep quiet about what he had seen that night and we never told anyone.'

'It's a good story, John,' said Edgar, listening to his friend as he finished his wine, 'a very good one. But now I really must be on my way home. I hope I don't meet any strange, thin men on the way.' The two men laughed, shook hands and went their different ways.

It was about a year later that Edgar, the listener to John's story, travelled to Ireland to visit another friend who lived in an old

'There was a terrible-looking man standing just outside
Sampson's window.'

country house there. One evening his host was looking in a box full of various old things for a key that he wanted. Suddenly he pulled a small object out of the box and held it up. 'Have a look at this, Edgar. What do you think it is?' he asked.

It was an old gold coin with the head of a king on the front. Edgar looked closely. 'Where did you get it?' he asked quietly.

'Well, it's quite an interesting story,' began his friend. 'A year or two ago we were working on that area of the garden over there in the corner, can you see? Among the four trees? Right in the middle of the trees, we found an old well and at the bottom of it, you'll never guess what we found.'

'Yes, I will. Was it a body, by any chance?' asked Edgar.

His friend was surprised. 'Yes, it was. In fact, we found two bodies. One of them had its arms tightly around the other. They were probably there for thirty years or more. Anyway, we pulled them out and in the pocket of one of them we found this old coin ... from Turkey or somewhere, by the look of it. It's got something on the back of it, too. Can you see what it says?'

'Yes, I think I can,' said Edgar. 'It seems to be the letters G. W. S. and the date 24 July 1865.'

Chapter 3   The Curtains
(*from* The Diary of Mr Poynter)

Mr James Denton's greatest love in life was books, old ones most of all. His collection grew bigger and bigger every year, but he lived in his aunt's house, and she was not very happy about this.

Mr Denton was in London one day to buy furniture for the new house which he and his aunt were building, and he was on his way to a shop to choose the curtains. His way took him, quite by chance, past one of the best bookshops in London, and he could not stop himself going in, just for a quick look, as he told himself.

He was just walking round the shop, looking at all the different books, when he noticed a small collection of books on the part of England that he came from, Warwickshire. He spent the next half an hour looking through these and finally decided to buy one that really interested him, called *The Diary of Mr Poynter, 1710*. He paid for the book and then, looking at his watch, he realized that he had very little time before his train back to Warwickshire left, and he had to rush to the station. He just caught the train.

That night, his aunt questioned him about his trip to London and was very interested to hear about the furniture which was going to arrive soon. Her nephew described everything in detail, but still she was not satisfied. 'And what about the curtains, James?' she asked. 'Did you go to ...?' Suddenly James remembered. 'Oh dear, oh dear,' he said, 'that's the one thing I missed. I am so sorry. You see, I was on my way there when, quite by chance, I passed Robins ...'

'Not Robins the bookshop, I hope,' cried his aunt. 'Don't

tell me you've bought more horrible old books, James.'

'Well, only one,' he said, feeling a bit guilty, 'and it's a very interesting one, a diary of someone who used to live not far from here ...' But he could see that his aunt was not really listening.

'You can't go to London again before next Thursday,' she was saying, 'and really, James, until we decide on the curtains, there's nothing more we can do.'

Luckily, she decided to go to bed soon after that and James was left alone with his new book, which he read until the early hours of the morning. He found this diary, with its stories of everyday life at that time, very interesting. The next day was Sunday. After church, James and his aunt sat in the living-room together.

'Is this the old book that made you forget my curtains?' asked his aunt, picking it up. 'Well, it doesn't look very good ... *The Diary of Mr Poynter*. Huh!' But she opened the book and looked at a few pages. Suddenly, much to his surprise, she began to show some interest. 'Look at this, James,' she said. 'Isn't it lovely?' It was a small piece of paper, pinned to one of the pages of the diary. On it was a beautiful drawing, made up of curving lines, which somehow caught the eye. 'Well, why don't we get it copied for the curtains if you like it so much?' he suggested, hoping that she would forgive him for his bad memory of the day before in London. His aunt agreed and the very next day, James took the piece of paper to a company in the nearest town, who agreed to copy it and make it into curtains.

About a month later, James was called in to inspect the work and was extremely pleased with the result. 'Was it a difficult job?' he asked the manager.

'Not too difficult, sir. But, to tell you the truth, the artist who did the work was very unhappy about it – he said there was something bad in the drawing, sir.' James was thoughtful but still he chose the colours for the curtains and then returned home. A

James, though, did not want to go to bed immediately and sat in the chair by the fire in his room, reading.

few weeks later, the curtains were ready and a man came to hang them in several rooms of the new house, one of which was James's bedroom. That night he found that he could not stop looking at them and, although it was a still night, he was almost sure that the curtains were moving and that someone was watching him from behind them. He told himself that this was impossible and not to be so stupid. He explained to himself that the effect was caused by the curving lines on the curtains, which looked just like long, curling black hair.

The next day, a friend of James's came to stay and after dinner they sat up late, talking and laughing. At last they decided to go to bed and James showed his friend to the guest room, which was just along from his own. James, though, did not want to go to bed immediately and sat in the chair by the fire in his room, reading. He fell asleep for a few minutes and, when he woke, he realized that something was in the room with him. Putting out his hand, he felt something covered in hair and thought it was his dog, who always followed him everywhere. 'How did you get in here? I thought I left you downstairs,' he said, looking down. To his horror, he found it was not his little dog, but something almost human. He jumped and screamed and, as he did, the face of the thing came up towards him: no eyes, no nose, no mouth. Only hair. He screamed again and rushed to the door, but was so frightened that he could not get it open. He felt the thing touch his back and start to tear at his shirt. At last the door flew open and he rushed to his friend's room, terrified and breathing hard.

The next morning, early, James went away to the seaside for a few days to try to forget about his horrible experience. He took with him *The Diary of Mr Poynter*. He wanted to read it again carefully to find out anything he could about the pattern pinned on to the page. When he turned to that part of the book he found that there were several pieces of paper stuck one on top of the other. He carefully pulled off the first two and found this story, written by Mr Poynter in 1707.

'Old Mr Casbury of Acrington told me this day of young Sir Everard Charlett, at that time a student of University College. The young man drank too much and broke the law many times, but because he was from an important family, the university never did anything about it. He used to wear his hair very long and curling down his neck and he wore unusual, colourful clothes. His behaviour made his father very unhappy. One day, they found young Sir Everard dead in his room, with all his hair pulled out. No one could explain why or how he died, but the strangest thing was that, the day after he died, the body disappeared completely, leaving only a pile of long, curling black hair on the floor of his room. His father kept some of this hair and had drawings made of it, part of which I have pinned to this page.'

This is the strange story behind the curtains. Before he returned home, James Denton ordered his servants to take them all down and burn them.

Chapter 4 The Flies

(*from* An Evening's Entertainment)

If you go to the end of the road, past Collin's house, on the left you will see a field with some old fruit trees in it. A little house used to be there where a man called Davis lived. He was a very quiet man who seemed to have enough money to live on. He didn't work on the farms, but he always went to town on market days. One day, a young man came back from market with him.

The young man was pale and thin, and he didn't speak very much. He lived with Mr Davis and nobody knew if he helped with the housework, or if Mr Davis was his teacher. But people talked and wondered why they were always walking together, early and late, up in the hills and down in the woods. They suspected that the two men were playing with magic and were plotting something terrible. Once a month, when the moon was full, they went up to a place on the hill where there are piles of old stones and rocks and they stayed up there all night. Someone once asked Mr Davis why he went to such a dark, lonely place in the middle of the night. Mr Davis smiled and replied, 'I love old places. They remind me of the past. And the air is beautiful on a summer's night. You can see all the countryside for miles around in the moonlight.'

But Mr Davis's young friend interrupted rudely: 'We don't want other people near us. We just want to talk to each other.'

Mr Davis seemed annoyed at his young friend's rudeness and he politely explained, 'People say that there are bodies under those old stones, the bodies of dead soldiers. I know farmers sometimes find old bones and pots when they are working in the fields around here. I'd like to know more about how those people lived and who their gods were. I think they probably practised magic.'

Then, one morning In September, something terrible

happened. A farm worker had to go up to the top of the hill, to the woods, very early, when it was still dark. In the distance he saw a shape that looked like a man in the early morning fog. As he came nearer, he saw that it *was* a man. It was Mr Davis's friend, dead, hanging from a tree. Near his feet was a knife, covered in blood. The poor farm worker was terrified and ran back down the hill to the village. He woke up some of the villagers to tell them about the terrible sight and some men went back up the hill with a horse to bring down the body. They also immediately sent a young boy to Mr Davis's house, to see if he was at home, because, of course, they suspected that he was the murderer. When they cut down the young man's body from the tree, they were surprised to see the clothes he was wearing were all black, like the clothes that vicars used to wear many centuries ago.

When the men's horse came near the tree and the dead young man, it screamed and tried to run away, but the men were able to hold it and they finally got back to the village with the body across the terrified horse's back. In the village they found the young boy standing in the main street, with several women standing around him. He was as white as paper and would not say a word. When the men tried to move on towards Mr Davis's house, the horse again became very frightened. It stopped in the road and would not move. Then suddenly it turned and tried to run, and the body of the dead young man fell off its back on to the road. The horse could smell blood. They carried the young man's body to Mr Davis's house and when they opened the door, they saw what the poor young boy had seen.

There, on the long kitchen table, was the body of Mr Davis. Tied round his eyes was a black handkerchief and his hands were tied behind his back. His chest was cut open from top to bottom and his heart was gone. It was an awful sight. The men ran outside for some fresh air – the smell of death in that room was so terrible. Later, they put the young man's body next to Mr Davis's and they looked carefully round the house. Why were these two men dead? How did they die? In one of the cupboards they found a small green bottle of strong medicine often used to put people to sleep.

'I think that young man gave Mr Davis some of this stuff to put him to sleep,' one man suggested, looking at the bottle, 'and then killed him. Goodness knows why. Perhaps he needed Davis's heart for his magic. Then later, perhaps, he was sorry about murdering his friend and went up the hill and killed himself.'

Well, the villagers decided that the two dead men could not lie in the graveyard near the church. 'They never came to church and they didn't believe in God,' they said. 'They believed in unnatural things, in magic.'

So twelve men covered the two bodies in black and took them to a place outside the village. There they dug a big hole, threw the bodies into it and covered them with stones. People say that

In the blood there were fat black flies, feeding.

horses don't like going near that place even today, and there is a strange kind of light there.

One day, some time later, some people walking along the road found a pool of blood across it. In the blood there were fat black flies, feeding. One man went to get some water and they washed the blood away, but the flies flew up into the air like a dark cloud, and flew towards Mr Davis's house. The villagers decided that no one should live in that house any more, so they set fire to it. The house burnt down completely, but for a long time people said that they often saw Mr Davis and the young man, standing at night when the moon was full, in the road near the burnt house on the hill.

Only the flies live there now. Perhaps it is only the flies who know why those two men played with magic and why they died the way they did.

Chapter 5   The Locked Room
(from Rats)

It happened in Suffolk, near the coast. There is a tall, red house there, built in about 1770, perhaps. It has a small, untidy garden behind it and from the front windows you can see the sea. Tall, dark trees stand around this lonely house. Near the front door there is a sign which shows that this was once a public house, where travellers could stop to eat and sleep.

One fine spring day, a young Cambridge University student called Thomson arrived at this house. He wanted to spend some time in a quiet and pleasant place where he could read and study. No one else was staying there at the time and Mr and Mrs Betts, who managed the house, welcomed him and made him feel very comfortable. They gave him a large room on the first floor with a good view from the window. He spent his days very calmly and quietly. Every morning he worked, he walked in the country in the afternoon, and he usually had a drink with some of the local people in the bar in the evening before going to bed. He was very happy to continue his life like this for as long as possible. He planned to stay for a whole month.

One afternoon, Thomson walked along a different road from the usual one and in the distance he saw a large white object. He walked towards it and discovered that it was a large square stone with a square hole in the middle. He examined the stone, then he looked at the view for a moment – the sea, the churches in the distance, the windows of one or two houses shining here and there in the sun – and he continued his walk.

That evening in the bar, he asked why the white stone was there. 'It's been there for a very long time, since before any of us were born, in fact,' said Mr Betts.

'People used to say that it brought bad luck ... that it was unlucky for fishing,' said another man.

'Why?' asked Thomson, but the people in the bar became silent and clearly didn't want to talk about the stone any more. Thomson was puzzled.

A few days later, he decided to stay at home to study in the afternoon. He didn't feel like going out for a walk, but at about three o'clock he needed a break. He decided to spend five minutes looking at the other rooms on his floor of the house – he was interested to know what they were like. He got up and went quietly out of his room, into the corridor. Nobody else was at home. 'They are all probably at market today,' he thought. The house was still and silent, except for the flies. The sun was shining and it was very hot. He went into the three rooms near his own bedroom; each one was pretty and clean. Then he tried the door of the south-west room, but found that it was locked. This made Thomson want to know why it was locked and what was inside it, and he took the keys of all the other doors on the floor to try to open it. He finally succeeded, the door opened, he went in and looked around him.

The room had two windows looking south and west, so it was very bright and hot. There were no carpets and no pictures, only a bed, alone in the corner. It was not a very interesting room, but suddenly ... Thomson turned and ran out of the room, closing the door behind him noisily.

'Someone was in there, in the bed!' he almost shouted. There were covers over the whole body on the bed, but it was not dead, because it moved. He was not dreaming, Thomson knew: this was the middle of a bright, sunny day, after all. He didn't know what to do.

First, of course, he had to lock the door again but, before he did this, he listened. Everything was silent inside the room. He put the key into the lock and turned it as quietly as he could, but

23

he still made some noise. Suddenly he stopped: someone was walking towards the door! He turned and ran along the corridor to his room, closed the door and locked it behind him as fast as he could. He waited and listened. 'Perhaps this person can walk through doors and walls?' he whispered to himself. Nothing happened.

'Now what?' he thought. His first idea was to leave the house as soon as he could, but if he changed his plans, Mr and Mrs Betts would know that something was wrong. Also, if they already knew about the person in the locked room but they still lived in the house, then there was surely nothing for him to be afraid of. Maybe it would be better to stay and say nothing. This was the easiest thing to do. Thomson stayed there for another week and, although he never went near the door again, he often stopped in the corridor and listened, but there was only silence. He didn't ask anyone in the village about the locked room because he was too afraid, but near the end of the week he started to think more and more about the person in the locked room and he eventually decided to find out more before he left. He made a plan – he would leave on the four o'clock train the next day and, while the horse waited outside with his bags, he would go upstairs and take one last, quick look into the room.

This is what happened. He paid Mr Betts, put the bags on the horse, thanked Mrs Betts and said, 'I'll just take a last look upstairs to be sure that I have all my things.' He then ran up the stairs and opened the door to the room as quietly as possible. He almost laughed. 'It's not a real person at all. How silly of me! It's just a pile of old clothes,' he thought. He turned to go, but suddenly something moved behind him. He turned quickly and saw the pile of old clothes walking towards him, with a knife stuck into the front of its jacket and dried blood all down its shirt. He pulled open the door and rushed out of the room

He turned to go, but suddenly something moved behind him.

and down the stairs. Then he fell and everything went black.

When he opened his eyes, Mr Betts was standing over him with a strong drink in a glass. He looked annoyed. 'You shouldn't have done that, Mr Thomson, sir. It was a stupid thing to do after we've been so good to you. Why did you want to look in that room? Nobody will want to stay in this house any more if you tell people what you've seen,' he said.

'I'm sorry. I just wanted to know, that's all,' said Thomson. 'I won't tell anyone, I promise.' So, before he left, Mr and Mrs Betts told him what they knew.

'People say that a rich gentleman lived here a long time ago. One evening, he was out walking in the village, when a group of men attacked him. They wanted to steal his money. They held him down on that big, white stone which you saw when you were out walking the other day and they killed him with a knife. Then they threw his body into the sea. Later some people from the village moved the stone away from the village; they said the fish along this part of the coast would not come anywhere near it. The fishermen were not catching anything, you see. The people who lived in this house before us told us to lock that bedroom but to leave the bed in it, because the gentleman's ghost might want to come back and sleep in the house again. You're the first person to see him since we've been here. He's never been a problem to us. But please don't tell anyone,' they repeated. 'We don't want people talking about ghosts in this house.'

For many years, Thomson didn't say a word to anyone about what happened in the Betts's house in Suffolk, and I only know his story because, years later, when he came to stay with my family, I was the person who showed him to his bedroom. When we reached the bedroom door, he opened it very loudly and stopped outside. He stood there for a minute and carefully inspected every corner of the room before he went in. Then he remembered that I was standing there and said, 'Oh, I'm sorry, my dear, but something very odd happened to me once.'

And he told me the story I have just told you.

Chapter 6   The Painting of —ngley Hall
(*from* The Mezzotint)

Mr S. Williams was a collector of paintings, and his special interest was pictures of old English country houses, English churches and country towns. One day, he received a price list from Mr Britnall's shop, where he often bought paintings. With the list was a note from Mr Britnall himself, saying that he thought painting number 978 might interest Mr Williams. Although the price seemed rather high, the description of number 978 made Mr Williams keen to see it. He decided to order it at once.

The painting arrived a few days later and Mr Williams tore off the paper, feeling quite excited. What he found was an ordinary picture of a large country house from the century before. The house had three rows of windows, there were tall trees on either side and a garden in front. The letters A. W. F. were in a corner of the painting, probably for the name of the artist. On the back of the picture was a piece of paper, torn in half, with the words '—ngley Hall, —ssex' on it. He could not see anything very special about the picture and could not understand why Mr Britnall thought he would like it or why the price was so high. He decided to send it back to the shop the next day.

That evening, a good friend, John Garwood, came to Williams's house and noticed the painting. 'A new one, eh, Williams? Mmm ... I rather like it. The light is very good and I rather like this person at the front,' he said.

'A person?' said Williams, coming closer. 'Oh yes, so there is! I didn't notice it before.' Only the head of the person could be seen. It was impossible to say whether it was a man or a woman, but it was standing under the dark trees at one side of the picture, looking at the house. 'And I suppose the light is quite good,'

Williams went on. 'I still feel it's a bit expensive, though. I was going to send it back tomorrow.'

Soon afterwards, the two men went out to dinner with some of their friends from the university and later Williams invited some of them back to his house for a drink. One of them, who was also interested in art, noticed the new painting. 'Quite interesting,' he said, 'but don't you find it rather horrible, Williams? The light is good, but that person standing in front of the house is rather frightening.'

Williams was too busy pouring drinks to look at the painting just then, but later, on his way to bed, he looked at it again and was amazed to see that the person in the picture was now right in front of the house, not to one side under the trees. The person seemed to be on their hands and knees, moving towards the house. He or she looked extremely thin and was dressed all in black, except for a white cross on the back.

'Am I going mad?' Williams asked himself. He decided to lock the picture in a cupboard but did not want to go straight to bed. 'I'll write down everything that has happened to the picture since it arrived here. Then in the morning I won't think this is all a dream,' he thought to himself. And that is what he did. He found it very difficult to sleep that night, and the next morning he decided to ask another friend, Nisbet to come and look at the painting.

'I want you to tell me exactly what you see in the picture, in detail,' he said to Nisbet, showing him the painting. 'I'll explain why afterwards.'

'Well, I can see a country house – English, I think – by moonlight . . .' began Nisbet.

'Moonlight?' interrupted Williams. 'Are you sure? There was no moon there when I first got it.'

Nisbet looked at his friend strangely. 'Shall I continue? The house has one – two –three rows of windows . . .'

The person seemed to be on their hands and knees, moving towards the house.

'But what about people?' interrupted Williams again.

'No one at all,' said Nisbet. 'But what *is* all this about, Williams?'

'I'll explain in a moment,' answered Williams. 'Can you see anything more?'

'Well, let me see, the only other interesting detail is that one of the windows on the ground floor is open,' said Nisbet.

'My goodness!' Williams shouted. 'It's inside the house now.' He rushed across the room to see for himself. Sure enough, Nisbet's description was correct. Williams went to his desk and wrote quickly for a minute or two. Then he brought two pieces of paper over to Nisbet. The first was a description of the painting as it was at that moment, which Nisbet signed. The second was Williams's description of the painting on the night before, which Nisbet read but did not believe.

'This is the strangest thing I've ever heard or seen,' said Nisbet. 'The first thing we must do is take a photograph of the painting before it changes again. Then we should try to find out where this place is in England. I feel there is something strange and terrible happening there.'

'Yes, and I also want to ask John Garwood to write a description of what he saw when he looked at the painting last night. We could only just see the person then, under the trees over on this side of the house,' said Williams, pointing at one side of the picture.

John Garwood came over immediately and, while he was writing his description, Nisbet photographed the painting. Then the three friends decided to go for a walk. 'Perhaps it will help us to think more clearly,' said Nisbet.

They returned to Williams's house at about five o'clock in the afternoon and were surprised to find Williams's servant, Robert, sitting and staring at the painting. When the three men entered, he jumped to his feet in embarrassment.

'I must apologize for sitting in your chair, sir,' he said to Williams. 'But I couldn't stop looking at this picture.'

'Please don't apologize, Robert. What do you think of the painting? I'm interested to hear your opinion,' said Williams.

'Well, sir. It's not the sort of painting I would let my young daughter look at. She's very easily frightened and I think this strange, thin person carrying a baby would give her bad dreams.'

The three men said nothing. They waited for Robert to go. As soon as the door closed, they rushed to the painting. Robert was right. The strange, bony person was now back in the picture, walking away from the house and, in its long, thin arms was a baby.

For two hours the three men sat and watched the picture, but it did not change again. They went to have dinner. After dinner

*The strange, bony person was now back in the picture, walking away
from the house and, in its long, thin arms was a baby.*

they came back again and by now the person was gone and the
house looked quiet and calm again in the moonlight.

They decided to read through books on Essex and Sussex to
find —ngley Hall. It was hard work, but many hours later, in a
Guide to Essex, Williams found the following information:

'The village of Anningley has an interesting twelfth-century
church and next to the church, in a beautiful park, stands Anningley
Hall, which used to be the country home of the Francis family. No
members of this family are now living; the last baby boy of the
family disappeared mysteriously in the middle of a September night
in 1802. Nobody could discover who took the baby but people
suspected that it was a member of the Gawdy family. Some time
before the baby disappeared, Tom Gawdy was caught stealing by Sir
John Francis, the father of the child, and Gawdy was hanged for his

crime. People say that the Gawdy family wanted revenge and that they took it by stealing the last child of the Francis family.'

'Well, it does seem that they got their revenge, if the story of our painting is true, doesn't it?' said Williams.

The painting has not changed again since then. It now hangs in the museum at Anningley, in Essex.

Chapter 7 Lost Hearts

In September of the year 1811, a little boy arrived at the door of Aswarby Hall in the middle of Lincolnshire. He rang the bell and looked around him at the tall, square eighteenth-century house. An evening light fell on the building, making the windows shine like fires. In front of the hall there was a park full of trees, and a church with a clock. It all seemed very pleasant to the boy as he waited for someone to open the door.

The boy's parents were dead and his elderly cousin, Mr Abney, wanted him to go and live at Aswarby. People who knew Mr Abney were surprised at his offer because they thought he was a man who loved books more than people and who preferred to live alone.

Mr Abney opened the door and seemed very happy to see his young cousin, Stephen Elliot. He immediately started to ask questions: 'How old are you, my boy? How are you? And how old are you? I mean, I hope you are not too tired to eat your supper?'

'No, thank you, sir,' said Stephen. 'I am quite well.'

'Good,' said Mr Abney. 'And how old are you, my boy?' It seemed strange that he asked the question twice in the first two minutes of their conversation.

'I'm twelve years old next birthday,' said Stephen.

'And when is your birthday, my dear boy? Eleventh of September, eh? That's good, that's very good. I like to write these things down in my book. Are you sure you will be twelve?'

'Yes, sir, quite sure.'

'Well, take him to Mrs Bunch's room, Parkes,' Mr Abney said to his servant, 'and let him have his supper.'

Mrs Bunch was the friendliest person at Aswarby. Stephen felt

34

Mr Abney opened the door and seemed very happy to see his young cousin, Stephen Elliot.

comfortable with her and they became good friends in a quarter of an hour. She was fifty-five years old and knew everything about the house and its neighbourhood. She was quite willing to share this information with Stephen and there were certainly many things about Aswarby Hall and gardens that the boy wanted to ask her.

♦

One November evening, Stephen was sitting by the fire in Mrs Bunch's room, thinking about his new home. 'Is Mr Abney a good man?' he suddenly asked.

'Good? My child!' said Mrs Bunch, 'He's the kindest man I've ever known! Haven't I told you about the little boy he brought here from the street seven years ago, and the little girl two years after I started working here?'

'No, please tell me about them, Mrs Bunch,' said Stephen.

'Well,' she began, 'I don't remember much about the little girl. Mr Abney brought her back from his walk one day and told Mrs Ellis to take care of her. The poor child had no family. She lived with us for about three weeks and then one morning she got up while everyone was still asleep and left the house. I've never seen her again. Mr Abney looked everywhere but she never came back. She was a very silent child but she helped me a lot and I loved her very much.'

'And what about the little boy?' asked Stephen.

'Ah, that poor boy!' said Mrs Bunch. 'He came here one winter day playing his music, and Mr Abney asked him lots of questions, such as "Where do you come from? How old are you? Where are your family?" He was very kind to the boy, but the same thing happened – he just disappeared.' That night Stephen had a strange dream. Near his bedroom at the top of the house there was an old bathroom, which nobody used. The top of the door was made of glass and it was possible to look in and see the bath. In his dream, Stephen looked through the glass and saw a body in the bath, a very thin, dusty body with a sad smile and the hands pressed over the heart. As Stephen looked, a terrible cry came from the lips, and the arms began to move. Stephen was extremely frightened and woke up suddenly. He found that he really was standing on the cold floor near the bathroom. Bravely, he looked through the glass again to see if the body was really there. It was not. He went back to bed.

When they heard about Stephen's experience, Mrs Bunch and Mr Abney were very interested and Mrs Bunch put a new curtain over the glass door of the bathroom. Mr Abney said he would write about Stephen's dream in his book.

♦

It was nearly spring when two more strange things happened. The first was that Stephen passed another very uneasy night and the next day he saw Mrs Bunch mending his night-shirt. She seemed rather angry with him, and asked 'How did you manage to tear your night-shirt so badly? It'll take me a long time to mend it.' Stephen looked and saw that there were some cuts in the shirt, a few inches long.

'I don't remember how it happened,' he said. 'I don't remember anything. But they're just the same as the scratches on the outside of my bedroom door.'

Mrs Bunch looked at him, her mouth open, and then ran upstairs to see. 'Well,' she said when she returned, 'It's very strange. I wonder how those scratches appeared . . . They're too high for a dog, a cat or a rat to make. Don't say anything to Mr Abney, but remember to lock your door when you go to bed tonight.'

'Oh, I always do,' replied Stephen.

The next evening, the second strange thing happened. Mr Parkes, the servant, visited Stephen and Mrs Bunch in Mrs

Bunch's room. He did not often come to see them there. When he came in, he didn't at first notice that Stephen was there. He seemed very nervous and uneasy. 'Mr Abney will have to get his own wine if he wants a drink in the evenings,' he said. 'If I can't go down and get it in the daytime, I won't go at all. There's something very strange down there under the house, you know – maybe it's the wind or maybe it's rats, but I don't think so . . . and I don't like it.'

'Don't talk like that,' answered Mrs Bunch. 'You'll frighten young Stephen.'

Mr Parkes suddenly noticed Stephen for the first time and quickly said, with a nervous laugh, 'Oh, I was only joking, you know.'

But Stephen knew that it wasn't a joke, and he was worried. He asked a lot of questions but Mr Parkes refused to tell him any more about the noises under the house.

◆

It was now March 24, 1812, a strange day, windy and noisy. Stephen stood in the garden and felt as if it was full of ghosts, people he couldn't see who were flying in the wind and trying to contact living people in the real world. After lunch that day, Mr Abney said, 'Stephen, my boy, will you come to my library late tonight at eleven o'clock? I will be busy until then but I want to show you something about your future life. Don't tell Mrs Bunch or anyone else in the house. Just go to your room at the usual time.' Stephen was excited. He could sit up until eleven o'clock! He looked in at the library door when he was on his way upstairs that evening and he saw on the table a silver cup filled with red wine, and an old piece of paper with words on it.

At about ten o'clock, Stephen was standing at the open window of his bedroom, looking out over the night-time countryside. The wind was not so strong now and there was a full moon. Suddenly he heard some strange cries – 'Perhaps someone lost in the night?' he thought. 'Or water birds down on the lake in the park?' The noises grew louder and came nearer the house. Then they stopped. But just as Stephen was about to close his window and continue reading his book, he saw two children standing outside under the dark trees, a boy and a girl. They stood together, looking up at his window. The girl reminded him of the girl in his dream about the bath. And the sight of the boy made him feel afraid. The girl was smiling, holding her hands over her heart. The boy, with his untidy black hair and old clothes, stretched his hands out helplessly in front of him. His fingernails were very long and dirty. As the boy stood there with his arms held out, Stephen suddenly saw something which made his hair stand on end. He could not believe his eyes. There, on the left side of the boy's chest, was a large black hole. Again Stephen heard the children's terrible, sad cries; then they disappeared. Although he was badly frightened, Stephen decided to go to Mr Abney's library. It was now nearly eleven o'clock. He walked very fast through the dark old house, quiet at this time of night with all the servants in bed. But when he arrived at the library, the door would not open. It was not locked and the key was on the outside, but when he knocked there was no answer. He listened carefully and he heard Mr Abney speaking . . . no, crying out. But why? Perhaps he too could see the strange children? Then, suddenly, everything was quiet and the library door opened by itself. Mr Abney was in his chair, his head thrown back and his eyes wide, with a look of terrible fear and pain on his face. On the left side of his chest was a large hole and Stephen could see his heart. But there was no blood on his hands and the long knife on the table was completely clean. The window of the library was open and the wind blew the curtains in a terrible dance. An old book was open on the table and this is what Stephen read:

'Thousands of years ago, people discovered that you could

*Stephen suddenly saw something which made his hair stand on end.
There, on the left side of the boy's chest, was a large black hole.*

control the world, fly, disappear or become someone or something else . . . all by magic. But to be able to use this magic, it is necessary first to take out the hearts of three young people, under twenty-one years of age. I have spent almost twenty years carefully choosing three young people who I could kill without anybody noticing. First was Phoebe Stanley on March 24, 1791. Second was an Italian boy, Giovanni Paoli, on March 23, 1805. And tonight, on March 24, 1812, the last child to die for me will be my cousin, Stephen Elliot. No one will ever find the bodies of these children. I have hidden the first two in my wine cellar, under the floor, and I will do the same with the third child tonight. The ghosts of these children may come back, the books tell me, crying horribly. They may try to take the heart of the man who killed them but this will not happen to me, I am sure.'
Stephen finished reading and looked at the body of his elderly cousin. Quietly, he left the room and closed the door.

◆

For many years people wondered about Mr Abney's death. 'It must have been a wild cat that came in through the open window and killed the poor man,' they said. But Stephen knew the truth.

Chapter 8   Martin's Lake

(*from* Martin's Close)

I was staying with a good friend of mine in the West Country. I arrived on the Friday night and my friend was keen to show me the village on the Saturday morning. 'I'll take you around and show you everything. Then I want you to meet a friend of mine, John Hill. He's about seventy years old and knows all the history of the village. Oh, and make sure you ask him about Martin's Lake.'

'Why? Is it a good place for fishing?' I asked.

He laughed. 'Well, no. There's no water in it now ... but let old John tell you the story. I'm sure you'll enjoy it,' said my friend.

The next day, after a tour of the village, we went to old John Hill's house for tea. We persuaded the old man to tell us the story of the lake:

'It was the Christmas of 1683 and a young gentleman, George Martin, returned from Cambridge University to the village. He was a popular young man and used to ride his horse long distances to visit his friends in the neighbourhood. One night it was snowing hard, so, instead of riding all the way to his house outside the village, he decided to stay at the small hotel here. As it was Christmas, there was music and dancing in the hotel and all the young men and women were dancing together, except one. Her name was Ann Clark, and she worked at the hotel. She was an innocent young girl, not very intelligent. In fact, people used to laugh at her behind her back and, of course, none of the young men wanted to dance with her. But George Martin, the young gentleman, took pity on her and asked her to dance. The band were playing an old song

42

called 'Lady, will you walk, will you talk with me?' Everyone saw how happy the poor girl was to have someone to dance with. Her face lit up with a smile.

After that night, the young gentleman came to the hotel every week. When he arrived on his horse, he used to sing that song and Ann Clark used to rush out to meet him as soon as she heard it. The two often went for walks together by the lake and some people say they saw them kiss.

This went on for a few months until George Martin's parents found a wife for him. She was a beautiful, rich young woman, and from a very good family. Everyone said how lucky George Martin was, but then it all went wrong. The young woman heard about Ann Clark and was angry that a gentleman like him went about with an ordinary country girl. She refused to marry him.

He, of course, regretted ever meeting Ann and was very angry to lose such a beautiful young wife. People say that the next time he saw Ann, they argued and he hit her. A week later, they were seen together again. He said a few words to her and then rode off. They say she looked very happy all that day but, not long after, she disappeared completely. No one could find her anywhere.

Some weeks later, George Martin came into the hotel again, went into the bar and asked for a drink. A young woman called Sarah, a friend of Ann Clark's, served him. 'Are you looking for Ann, sir?' she asked. 'Because no one has seen her for weeks.' He answered angrily that, no, he was not looking for her and he sat alone, drinking his beer. Sarah started to wash some glasses and, without thinking, began to sing the song, 'Lady, will you walk, will you talk with me?' The young gentleman's face turned pale and he told her to stop singing immediately. She stopped immediately, of course, but then suddenly, she heard Ann's voice outside the door, continuing the song. 'It's

Ann! She's back!' Sarah cried and ran towards the door.

'Stop!' shouted George Martin, but it was too late. The door opened and a strong, cold wind blew out all the lamps, leaving the room completely dark. Sarah heard someone walk across the floor, and the door of the big cupboard opened and shut. When she lit the lamps again, she saw something that looked like the bottom of a woman's dress caught under the cupboard door. Sarah was frightened and asked one of the men in the bar to open the cupboard. As the man pulled open the cupboard door, George Martin screamed and ran out of the bar into the street. Out of the cupboard came a small human shape, dressed in clothes that looked wet. No one saw its face, but everyone felt a freezing wind as it passed through the bar and into the darkness outside.

The next person to see George Martin was a young boy, who was coming home from fishing at the lake. He said he saw the young gentleman running towards the water, looking very frightened. He broke a branch off a tree and started to feel around in the water with it. After some minutes, the branch hit something and a strange sound like a scream came from deep in the lake. George Martin covered his ears with his hands and started to scream also. As he did, the boy saw a human shape come out of the water and chase the young gentleman away into the trees.

The boy ran and called the police. They found the body of Ann Clark at the bottom of the lake and under a tree was George Martin's knife, covered in blood. He was guilty of murder, of course, and they hanged him five weeks later. After that, everyone knew it as Martin's Lake, although it's dry now. And, do you know,' said old John Hill, 'that even now no one will sing that song in this village. People say it's unlucky.'

Sarah was frightened and asked one of the men in the bar to open the cupboard.

Chapter 9   The Two Cousins
(*from* The Tractate Middoth)

One autumn afternoon, an elderly man entered a library, showing a card with his name on it – Mr John Eldred – and asked if he could borrow a book. 'The name of the book I want is *The Tractate Middoth* – it's number 11334, I believe,' he said. 'But I don't know this library at all. Would someone be able to go and find it for me?' A young man who worked there, Mr Garrett, was passing and he answered, 'Of course, I'll go and find it for you immediately, sir.' Mr Eldred sat down on a chair near the door to wait.

When Mr Garrett returned he had to apologize for failing to find the book. 'I'm very sorry, Mr Eldred, but someone has already borrowed that book.'

'Are you sure?' replied Mr Eldred.

'Yes, sir,' said Garrett, 'but if you wait a moment you'll probably meet the man who has taken it as he leaves the library. I didn't see him very well but I think he was an elderly man, quite short, wearing a black coat.'

'It's all right,' said Mr Eldred, 'I won't wait now, thank you. I have to go. But I'll come back again tomorrow and perhaps you can find out who has the book?'

'Of course,' replied Garrett, and Eldred left the library quickly.

Garrett thought, 'I'll just go back to that room and see if I can find the old man. I'll ask him if he can wait a few days for the book and then I'll give it to Mr Eldred tomorrow.' So he went back to the same room and, when he got there, the book – *The Tractate Middoth* – was back in the right place.

Garrett felt very bad. 'Mr Eldred hasn't got the book he wants,' he said to himself, 'because I didn't see it. I'll wait for him tomorrow and give him the book myself.'

The next morning, he was waiting for Mr Eldred. 'I'm very sorry,' he said when Eldred came in, 'but I was sure that the old man took the book away with him. If you'll wait for a moment, I'll run and get it for you now.' Again Eldred sat down and waited, but this time his wait was very long. After twenty minutes he asked the woman behind the front desk if it was very far to the part of the library where Garrett was looking for the book.

'No, not far at all, sir,' she answered. 'It's odd that he's taking such a long time,' and she went to look for Garrett. She came back a few minutes later, looking rather worried. 'I'm very sorry, sir, but something has happened to Mr Garrett,' she said. 'He suddenly became ill while he was looking for your book and we have had to send him home.'

Mr Eldred was surprised but he answered politely, 'I'm so sorry that Mr Garrett became ill while he was trying to help me. I'd very much like to go to his house to ask how he is. Could you give me his address?'

The woman gave him the address and, before he left, Eldred asked her one last question. 'Did you see an elderly man in a black coat, leaving the library soon after I was here yesterday afternoon?'

'No, I didn't,' replied the woman. 'There were only two or three other men in here yesterday afternoon and they were all quite young, I think.'

Mr Eldred then left for Mr Garrett's house. He found him in a chair by the fire, looking pale and ill. 'I'm so sorry for all the trouble I have caused you,' Garrett said.

'Don't worry about it,' said Eldred. 'But what happened in that room? Did you fall? Did you see something?'

'Well, yes, I *did* fall and it *was* because I saw something,' answered Garrett. 'It was just as I went into the room where we keep that book you want ...'

'No, no,' said Eldred hurriedly. 'Don't tell me now. You will make yourself ill again.'

'But I'd like to tell someone,' answered Garrett.

'Not now, young man, not now,' said Eldred, standing up quickly. 'I'm afraid I must go now,' and he moved towards the door. Garrett gave him the exact number of the book, *The Tractate Middoth*, so that he could go to the library and find it himself the next day. But Eldred did not appear at the library again.

Garrett had another visitor later that day – George Earle, who worked with him. George said, 'I'm sure there is something odd going on at the library, you know. When we found you on the floor there was a terrible, strong smell in that room. It can't be good for people to work with a smell like that.'

Garrett replied, 'That smell isn't always there. I've only noticed it during the last few days. And it wasn't the smell that made me ill. It was something I saw . . . let me tell you about it. I went into that room this morning to get a book for a man who was waiting downstairs, a Mr Eldred. The afternoon before, I saw a short, old man in black take the same book out, but when I looked again the book was there, back in its place. So this morning, I went back to get it for Mr Eldred, but the same old man in black was there again. I looked more closely at him this time and saw that his skin was dry and brown and dusty. He had no hair at all. Horrible, he was; really ugly. He was reading a book near the one I wanted and when he turned round I saw his face . . . and he had no eyes! It was a terrible shock. Everything suddenly seemed to go black inside my heard and I fell. I can't tell you anything more.'

Before Garrett returned to work, his boss at the library told him to take a week off, go away somewhere and get some fresh air, to try to forget his experience. So he went to the station, carrying his luggage, and waited for a train to Burnstow-on-Sea. As the train arrived, only one car seemed to have any places in it,

'When he turned round I saw his face … and he had no eyes!'

but as he walked towards it, the head of the old man with no eyes suddenly appeared again at the window of the train. Garrett felt sick. He ran to the next car and jumped into it just as the train started to move. The next thing he knew was that a woman and her daughter were kindly helping him to sit down. They seemed rather worried about him. Mrs Simpson and her daughter were also travelling to Burnstow-on-Sea. They had an apartment there and during the journey they invited Garrett to stay with them. They soon became friends and spent a lot of time together. On the third evening of his stay, when Garrett was telling them about his work at the library, the daughter suggested that Garrett might be able to help them with a problem they had.

'Yes,' said her mother. 'We'll tell Mr Garrett our story and perhaps he'll be able to help us.'

'I'll certainly try,' answered Garrett.

'Well,' began Mrs Simpson, 'I had an old uncle called Dr Rant, and when he died he left directions that we should put his body in a special underground room under a field near his house, and that he should wear his ordinary clothes. Since then, many of the country people around there say that they have seen him in his old black coat. Anyway, he's been dead for twenty years now. He had no wife or family – just me, his niece, and my cousin John. He had a lot of money and a big house and John and I hoped to receive half each when he died. But the day before he died, I was sitting near his bed when he suddenly opened his eyes and said, "Mary, I've left everything to John in my will, you know. You won't get anything when I die." This was a shock to me, because my husband and I were not rich and we needed the money, but I said nothing because I felt that he wanted to say something more. I was right. He continued, "But, Mary, I don't like John and I think my will is wrong. I've decided that you should have everything ... but first you'll have to find the letter in which I have written my new will and I'm not going to tell you where it is. But I will tell you one thing – I've left it in a book, Mary, and the book is not in this house. It's in a place where John can go and find it any time. So, I'll tell you something more that John doesn't know. When I'm dead you'll find an envelope in my desk with your name on it and inside it you'll find something that will help you." Well, a few hours later, he died and I wrote to my cousin John Eldred, but of course, he has never replied. Meanwhile, we have to continue living in our small apartment here at Burnstow-on-Sea.'

'Did you say John Eldred?' asked Garrett, amazed. 'I saw a man called John Eldred just a few days ago. A thin, elderly man.'

'Yes, that sounds like him. Where did you see him?' asked Mrs Simpson.

'In a public place,' said Garrett. 'I don't know if I should tell you where. But what about the envelope?'

'Here it is,' answered Mrs Simpson. And she took out a small piece of paper with just five numbers on it – 11334. Garrett thought for a moment and then asked, 'Do you think Mr Eldred knows exactly *where* the book is which contains your uncle's letter?'

'Well, I don't know. People say he's always going to libraries and bookshops, so he must know its name, but probably not *where* it is,' answered Mrs Simpson.

Garrett was silent as he thought about the problem.

The next day, Garrett left Burnstow-on-Sea and travelled home by train. He couldn't remember if the book Mr Eldred wanted so badly had the same library number as the one on Mrs Simpson's piece of paper, but he knew there were three possibilities: 1.13.34, 11.33.4 or 11.3.34. As soon as the train arrived he went to the library to look. 11.33.4 was in the right place, but 11.3.34 was not there. He ran to the front desk and asked the woman there, 'Has anyone taken out book number 11.3.34?'

'How would I know? Do you think I can remember all the numbers of books people take out?' the woman replied.

'Well, has Mr Eldred been back here – you know, the old man who was here the day I became ill?'

'No, he hasn't been back here himself, but he did send me some money and asked me to send him a book. I couldn't refuse, of course. What would you do if someone sent you money and asked you to do such a thing?'

'I suppose I would do the same. Could you show me the ticket Mr Eldred sent and give me his address, please?'

'Here's the ticket,' said the woman. 'The book is number 11.3.34. Isn't that the number you just said you wanted? I'm afraid I didn't keep the address.'

'When did you send the book?' asked Garrett.

'At half past ten this morning.'

'Good, it's only one o'clock now,' he thought. But how could he get the address? He thought quickly and then remembered that John Eldred was living in his uncle's house, the house that Mrs Simpson and her daughter knew was really theirs. 'And if the dead uncle gave the book with that letter inside it to this library, then it must be on our list. And I know that he died about twenty years ago,' thought Garrett. So, he found the list and turned back to 1870. There it was: 14 August 1875, *The Tractate Middoth*. Given by Doctor J. Rant of Bretfield House.

Garrett looked for Bretfield House on a map. It was about a two-hour train journey away, he found. He left immediately for the station and caught the train, thinking all the time about what he was going to say to Mr Eldred about the book and about why he wanted to take it back with him. When he arrived at Bretfield Station, he started walking quickly towards the house, hoping that he would arrive there before the book did.

Suddenly, Garrett saw a taxi with two men in it, just leaving the station, going in the same direction as he was. He recognized

*He was just about to tear a page from the book when suddenly
something small and dark ran out from behind a tree.*

John Eldred and thought to himself, 'He's been to the station to
collect the book which the library sent him this morning.' He
stopped and looked towards the taxi. Eldred was getting out of it
and the driver was moving away slowly up the road. Eldred
followed it on foot. As he walked, something fell from his pocket:
a box of matches. He continued walking.

It was getting dark; the light was going now. Eldred was
walking slowly but Garrett could see that he was turning the
pages of the book, looking for something. He then stopped and
felt in all his pockets; he looked annoyed when he found that the
box of matches was not there. He was just about to tear a page
from the book when suddenly something small and dark ran out
from behind a tree. Two strong black arms caught him round the
head and neck. There was no sound; Eldred fought wildly but

silently with his arms and legs. Then it was over. Eldred lay there alone on the road. Garrett shouted and started to run towards the body. Another man who was working in a field near the road, ran over to help, but Eldred was already dead.

Later, the police and the lawyers asked Garrett many questions but he could only repeat, 'Someone attacked Mr Eldred just as he was going to tear a page from his book.'

They soon found, of course, that on the same page there was a lot of writing by old Doctor Rant, which said that his house and all his money really belonged to Mrs Mary Simpson and not to John Eldred. And it is not very difficult to imagine how William Garrett was soon able to leave his job at the library to become the next owner of Bretfield House, with his wife, Mrs Simpson's daughter.

ACTIVITIES

Chapter 1–3

Before you read

1 Find these words in your dictionary. They are all in the story.
*ash-tree behaviour Bible chapter grave graveyard
horror host pattern terrified vicar well witch*
Which word or words answer these questions? (You will have to
use one word twice.)
  a Which four words might you find in or near a church?
  b Which word appears thousands of times in a library?
  c Which two words are about feelings?
  d Something which is repeated many times is a . . . . . .
  e Which two words are very different types of people?
  f Which word might you read in a child's school report?
  g Which word might you see in a wood?
  h Which word is a person giving a party?
  i Which word means a place where you can get water from?
2 The stories in this book are all horror stories. The first one is called
  'The Ash-Tree'. How do you think a tree could be frightening?
3 The kind of school where pupils live all the time is called a
  boarding school. Do you think these schools are a good idea? Why
  or why not?
4 'The Curtain' is part of a longer story called *The Diary of My
  Poynter*. What connection do you think there might be between a
  diary and something as ordinary as curtains?

After you read

5 In 'The Ash-Tree', how do Sir Matthew and Sir Richard die and
  where are they found?
6 At the end of 'A School Story' two dead bodies are found in the
  well. Who are they?
7 In 'The Curtains', James thinks his little dog has followed him into
  the bedroom, but he is wrong. What is it?

Chapters 4–6

Before you read

8 Check the word *corridor* in your dictionary. For writers this can often be a convenient place in a story – why?

9 Horror stories are often about animals and insects. List horror films you have seen and horror stories you have read.

10 Why is the idea of a locked room so interesting? What do you think might be inside the room in this story?

11 Paintings of people can be frightening but how do you think a painting of a house might frighten you?

After you read

12 In 'The Flies', why do the people in the village decide that the bodies of Mr Davis and his friend can't lie in the graveyard of the church?

13 In 'The Locked Room', who says:
   a 'People used to say that it brought bad luck …'
   b 'Someone was there, in the bed!'
   c 'It was a stupid thing to do after we've been so good to you.'

14 a How many times does the picture change in 'The Painting of —ngley Hall'?

   b How is the painting different at the end of the story to when Williams first sees it?

Chapters 7–9

Before you read

15 Look up the word *truth* in your dictionary. Telling a ..... is the opposite of telling the truth. Now write a sentence including both words.

16 Check the meaning of the noun *will* in your dictionary. A will is always private until something happens. What must happen before other people can read it?

17 Why do you think a lake might be named after a person?

After you read

18 In the story 'Lost Hearts', what does Stephen see in his dream?

19 In the story of 'Martin's Lake' two people sing the same song, 'Lady will you walk, will you talk with me?' Who are they?

20 In 'The Two Cousins', who says:

   a 'Did you see an elderly man in a black coat, leaving the library soon after I was here yesterday afternoon?'

   b 'It can't be good for people to work with a smell like that.'

   c 'People say he's always going to libraries and bookshops, so he must know its name, but probably not *where* it is.'

Writing

21 Write about the story you enjoyed most, describing what it is about and why you liked it.

22 Look at the picture on page 35. Describe the two characters in the picture.

23 All these stories happened a long time ago. Which one do you think could easily be written again, in the present? What changes would you make to it?

24 In 'A School Story', John tells Edgar a story about a gold coin that belonged to his Latin teacher, when John was a boy. A year after he hears this story, Edgar sees the same coin. Write Edgar's letter to John explaining how and where he has seen the coin.

25 When Sir Richard Fell decides to rebuild the local church in 'The Ash-Tree', some of the graves have to be moved. One is the grave of Mrs Mothersole, who was hanged forty years earlier as a witch. Imagine you are one of the villagers watching as Mrs Mothersole's grave is opened. Explain what you see and how you feel.

26 Which story do you find the most frightening? Why? What do you think makes a good ghost or horror story?

Answers for the Activities in this book are available from your local office or alternatively write to: Penguin Readers Marketing Department, Pearson Education, Edinburgh Gate, Harlow, Essex CM20 2JE.